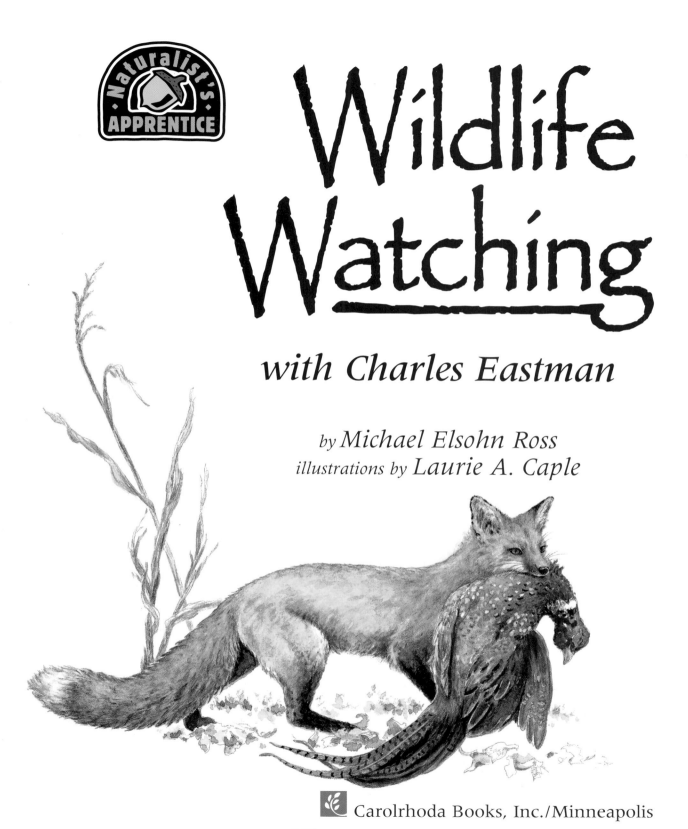

Wildlife Watching

with Charles Eastman

by *Michael Elsohn Ross*
illustrations by Laurie A. Caple

Carolrhoda Books, Inc./Minneapolis

To my brother naturalist, David Kirkpatrick—M.E.R.

To my parents, Dennis and Elizabeth Anderson—L.A.C.

Many thanks to Eastman scholar Kent Nerburn and David O. Born, professor and chair of the department of American Indian Studies at the University of Minnesota, for their help with this book.

Text copyright © 1997 by Michael Elsohn Ross
Illustrations copyright © 1997 by Laurie A. Caple
Photographs courtesy of: State Historical Society of North Dakota/Frank B. Fiske, cover, p. 42; © YMCA of the USA, Chicago, Illinois, p. 4; Smithsonian Institution, National Anthropological Archives, neg. no. 3195–f–1, p. 18; Dartmouth College Library, pp. 20, 21; Sophia Smith Collection, Smith College, p. 23; Western History Collections, University of Oklahoma Library, p. 24; the Jones Library, Inc., Amherst, Massachusetts, pp. 25, 36; James and Miriam Dayton, pp. 27, 28; UPI/Corbis-Bettmann, p. 35.

Carolrhoda Books, Inc., c/o The Lerner Publishing Group
241 First Avenue North, Minneapolis, MN 55401 U.S.A.

LIBRARY OF CONGRESS CATALOGING-IN-PUBLICATION DATA

Ross, Michael Elsohn, 1952-
    Wildlife watching with Charles Eastman / by Michael Elsohn Ross ; illustrations by Laurie A. Caple.
        p.   cm.
    Includes index.
    Summary: Presents a biography of Charles Eastman, the Native American physician, writer, and naturalist, focusing on his study of animals and their behavior. Provides tips on how to observe neighborhood wildlife.
    ISBN 1-57505-004-8
    1. Wildlife watching—Juvenile literature. 2. Eastman, Charles Alexander, 1858–1939—Juvenile literature.
[1. Wildlife watching. 2. Eastman, Charles Alexander, 1858–1939. 3. Santee Indians—Biography. 4. Indians of North America—Great Plains—Biography. 5. Naturalists.] I. Caple, Laurie A., ill. II. Title. III. Series: Ross, Michael Elsohn, 1952–   Naturalist's apprentice.
QL60.R655 1997
599—dc20   96-11470

Manufactured in the United States of America
1 2 3 4 5 6 – JR – 02 01 00 99 98 97

Contents

RIVER OTTERS

American Robin

Gray Squirrel

Chapter 1
Child of the Woods

Have you ever listened to the conversations of crows or toads? Maybe you've watched a lizard sunbathing on a rock or a raccoon sneaking about in the twilight. Are you curious about the actions of your animal neighbors? Do you wonder how squirrels talk or why chipmunks are so nervous? Does animal watching fill you with questions? Imagine spending your whole life untangling the mysterious behavior of all sorts of wild creatures. Fancy yourself becoming a world-famous wildlife watcher.

Over one hundred years ago, in 1858, a baby boy began to learn about the other creatures that shared his wooded home near what later became Redwood Falls, Minnesota. Wrapped snugly in an oak cradle, young Hakadah swayed in the soft summer breeze. His grandmother, Uncheedah, had hung his cradle like a bird's nest from a wild grapevine while she worked about their camp. (*Uncheedah* is the Sioux word for "grandmother.") As birds and squirrels hopped about the nearby branches, Hakadah babbled in a strange baby talk that sounded quite a bit like the voices of his wild friends. The curious animals watched him carefully, and sometimes birds even landed on the hood of the cradle for a closer visit. Perhaps they sensed that the baby would become an important **naturalist** and spend his life studying and loving nature.

Squirrels (part of the family Sciuridae)

28 species of squirrels in North America. The Sciuridae family also includes marmots, chipmunks, prairie dogs, and woodchucks.

Habitat: grasslands, forests, and deserts

Habits: Most species are diurnal, or active during the day. Some hibernate, or sleep through the entire winter.

Nests: in ground burrows or tree cavities

Diet: seeds, fruit, insects, and meat

FOX SQUIRREL

CHICKAREE

Hakadah's mother, Mary Nancy Eastman, had died shortly after his birth. She was the daughter of Seth Eastman, a U.S. Army captain, and Stands Sacred, the daughter of a Dakota chief. As she was dying, one of the medicine men caring for her said of her newborn child, "Another medicine man has come into existence, but the mother must die. Therefore let him bear the name 'Mysterious Medicine.'" However, one of the baby's uncles already bore that name, and the child was his mother's last, so he was named Hakadah, which means "pitiful last," instead. (Dakota babies were often given names that reflected their place in the family.) After his mother's death, Hakadah lived with his father, Many Lightnings, and was cared for by his grandmother, Uncheedah, who was also from an important Dakota family.

The Dakota are a nation of many peoples who speak the same language. *Dakota* means "allied people." They once lived from the wooded lake region of Minnesota to the plains of Wyoming. Europeans called them the Sioux. Although the Dakota preferred to be called "Dakota," gradually they too started using the name "Sioux."

Sioux mothers were responsible for introducing their children to the wonders of nature. Uncheedah, though sixty years old, gladly took on this role. To her, the birds were powerful spirits who lived close to the "Great Mystery" (a higher power not unlike the Holy Spirit in the Christian faith). Whenever she heard a birdsong, she would tell her grandson about it. "Hakadah," she would say, "listen to Shechoka [the robin] calling his mate. He says he has just found something good to eat." Or "Listen to Oopehanska [the thrush]; he is singing for his little wife. He will sing his best."

One of the most important things Uncheedah taught Hakadah was the art of being quiet. This would protect him during raids by enemy tribes, such as the Ojibway, because he could remain hidden. When he got older, it helped him lie in wait for game (animals hunted for food). At the same time, he was able to watch wild creatures and learn more about them without scaring them off.

Becoming an Invisible Observer

Do your parents ever call you a human tornado? Acting wild and crazy is part of being a kid. As a young child, Hakadah ran about just like you do, but he also knew how to blend into the woods like a quiet fawn. Would you like to become an ignored and unnoticed watcher of wild beasts? To get started, check out the tips below.

✔ Splash Your Face

To perk up every morning, the Sioux would splash their faces with cold water or even take a dip in a frigid lake or river. Awaken your senses before you go outside to watch wildlife so you won't fall asleep on the job!

✔ A Bump on a Log

Breathing slowly and deeply is really relaxing. Find someplace quiet in your backyard or another outdoor locale where you can be by yourself. Sit down with your back straight. If you are on a soft surface, such as a lawn, you may choose to lie down. If there are any shrubs around, camouflage yourself by sitting among the branches and shadows. Once you're settled, silently count to six as you take a deep breath. Let it out slowly, and repeat the process a few more times. This should help you feel calm and keep you from fidgeting. (In the summer, insect repellent might help too!) Though a friend passing by may notice you, if you stay still for a few minutes, birds and other creatures may see you as nothing but a bump on a log.

✔ Silent Watcher

Keep your eyes and ears wide open. Perhaps you'll notice a gopher poking out of its burrow or a bird singing from the shadows. Relax, and sights will come your way!

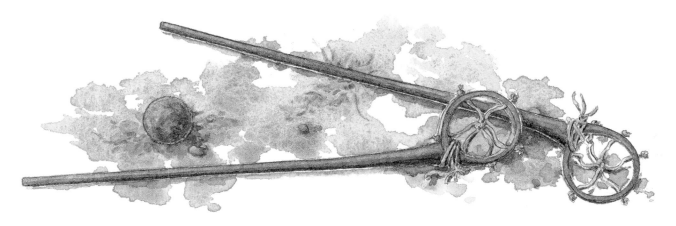

Even as a very young boy, Hakadah did not like his name. He didn't want to be thought of as pitiful. Then, in the summer of 1862, the four-year-old was given a chance at a new name. Having more than one name wasn't unusual among the Sioux people. Special events and heroic deeds might earn someone a new name, as could a resemblance to a respected animal. During the midsummer festival, Hakadah's band, or group of Sioux families, was to play another band in a game of lacrosse. Lacrosse is like a cross between soccer and hockey. Using sticks with a basketlike cup on the end, players try to pass and carry a ball to the opponents' goal. Hakadah's band chose him as their mascot for the game. A medicine man announced that if their band won, Hakadah would be given the name Ohiyesa, "the winner."

Both teams played hard that day, but finally Hakadah's band snagged the ball and made a goal. Cheers rose up in the victors' camp, and both teams gathered in a large circle. Little Hakadah, overwhelmed by all the ruckus, was led into the middle as the crowd called out "Ho-o-o" in approval. Then the old medicine man turned to the boy and announced, "Ohiyesa shall be your name henceforth. Be brave, be patient and you shall always win! Your name is Ohiyesa." The small boy now had a name to be proud of.

Shortly after this event, Ohiyesa's bravery was tested. The Eastern Sioux were having difficult times. Minnesota had been filling with white settlers for years. In 1851, the newcomers had tricked the Sioux into signing a treaty, or agreement, in which they gave up most of their land for the promise of yearly payments from the United States government. With less land in which to hunt, many of the Sioux were forced to become farmers. But during the summer of 1862, a drought caused their crops to fail. On top of this, the government was not giving them the money and supplies that it had promised in the treaty. The Sioux people were hungry, and many of the young men were angry.

In August, against the wishes of most of the tribe, some of the young men decided it was a good time to take back some of their tribal lands. The American Civil War was raging in the East, and many pioneers had left to fight with the Union army. The group of young Sioux killed settlers and attacked army forts, and they were soon captured. But many Sioux, including Ohiyesa's family, feared punishment for the deeds of these men and fled north to Canada. Uncheedah, Mysterious Medicine, Ohiyesa, and his brother Chatanna made it safely. Ohiyesa's father, Many Lightnings, and Ohiyesa's other two brothers were separated from the rest of the family during the confusion. Along with more than a thousand other Sioux men, women, and children, the men were captured and put on trial for the murders of the settlers. Later Ohiyesa heard that his father was one of many warriors hanged by the army in revenge.

Now without mother or father, four-year-old Ohiyesa bravely settled into a new life in unknown territory. As hunters and gatherers of food such as wild rice, the family moved often and sometimes had to set up camp in the territory of unfriendly tribes.

Almost every day, Ohiyesa explored the woods with Chatanna. Like other Sioux boys, they were well equipped for outdoor adventures. Dressed in comfortable, loose-fitting buckskin pants and shirts, the boys were able to climb trees and crawl through brush without getting scratched. The light brown buckskin camouflaged them as they hid in the shadowy woods. The moccasins on their feet allowed them to walk as quietly as a cat. In their hands they each carried a bow, and over one shoulder they slung a quill full of arrows.

You don't have to dress just like Chatanna and Ohiyesa to be a wildlife watcher, but you might want to think about how to equip yourself for your next trip.

The Well-Equipped Wildlife Watcher

sun hat

clothes that blend into your surroundings

loose pants for walking ease

sturdy shoes

binoculars

hand lens

belt pouch with pencil and notebook, water, and sunblock

field guide

COMMON IGUANA
(40-79 INCHES)

When Ohiyesa and Chatanna returned from their outings, their little cousin, Oesedah, often bombarded them with questions. Even though she was younger, Ohiyesa respected her wisdom. Sometimes their grandmother would lead the two in long discussions about the natural world. "To what tribe does the lizard belong?" asked Uncheedah one time.

"To the four-legged tribe," shouted Ohiyesa.

"It belongs to the creeping tribe," argued Oesedah.

The Sioux classified animals into four basic groups: those that walk on four legs, those that fly, those that swim, and those that creep. Ohiyesa asked his grandmother the difference between walking and creeping. Uncheedah replied that a walking animal keeps its body above the ground, while a creeper drags its body. The argument continued as the two children supported their opinions with facts. Finally, Ohiyesa went out and found a lizard. He and Oesedah smoothed the ground and covered it with ashes so they could see the tracks. How do you think they classified the lizard after they had seen it walk?

Lizards (suborder Lacertilia)

Over 2,500 species in the world

Habitat: grasslands, forests, and deserts

Habits: Most are diurnal, but some are nocturnal and come out at night. In cold climates, they are inactive during winter and rest under bark or rocks.

Diet: insects

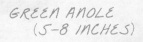

GREEN ANOLE
(5-8 INCHES)

Choosing and Using a Field Guide

When Ohiyesa realized that a lizard really does drag its belly as it walks, he quickly agreed that it belonged to the creeping tribe. As you notice creatures on your own, perhaps you too will wonder what they are called or what group they belong to. Unlike Ohiyesa, you may not have someone like Uncheedah to teach you their names. Luckily, many books are available in libraries and bookstores that can introduce you to your neighborhood wildlife. There are separate field guides for different groups, such as mammals, birds, and reptiles. Here are some tips to help you select the most useful guide.

✔ Illustrations vs. Photos

Believe it or not, a drawing or painting usually shows more detail than a photo. Go for a book with illustrations.

✔ The Whole Gang

Find a book that includes all the **species,** or kinds, of animals that live in your region, not just the common ones. Otherwise you'll be clueless if an uncommon creature pays a visit.

✔ User-Friendly

Choose a guide that is easy to use. If pictures and descriptions are all on one page, you'll be better able to make a quick ID while the animal is still in sight.

✔ In the Pocket

A book that can fit in your back pocket or belt pouch is just the right size. Imagine trying to use binoculars when you are carrying a book in your hand, or having to dig your guide out of your backpack every time you see an animal. It won't wait around for you to get your act together!

SNOWY OWL

✔ Get the Facts

The first few times you go wildlife watching, simply flip through your field guide until you find a picture that matches each animal you see. As you become more familiar with your guide and the creatures around you, you might recognize an animal as a member of the squirrel, skunk, or fox family. Then you'll be able to turn right to that section of the guide. Keep the book in a handy place where you can flip through it regularly.

Soon you'll be able to make lightning-quick identifications.

STRIPED SKUNK

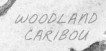

WOODLAND CARIBOU

At the age of eight, Ohiyesa was ready to learn the ways of a warrior and hunter. To teach him to be alert, his uncle Mysterious Medicine would wake him from his morning sleep with a loud war cry. After many a startling wake-up call, Ohiyesa learned to jump out of bed with his weapons in hand, responding with a war cry of his own. To teach him to endure hard times, Mysterious Medicine would make him go without food for a whole day. To teach bravery, he sent Ohiyesa out to get water in the middle of the night, even when they were in enemy territory. Most importantly, Mysterious Medicine helped Ohiyesa become aware of the minute details of nature. Without this knowledge, he would never become a successful hunter.

"Look closely [at] everything you see," Mysterious Medicine would say before Ohiyesa left the tepee for the day.

In the evening, there would be a quiz. "On which side of the trees is the lighter-colored bark? On which side do they have the most regular branches?" his uncle might ask.

Ohiyesa would also have to list all the birds he had encountered that day. If he didn't know the names, he would describe what they looked like, how their song sounded, or maybe what kind of nest they had.

"You ought to follow the example of Shunktokecha [the wolf]," Mysterious Medicine would remind him often. "Even when he is surprised and runs for his life, he will pause to take one more look at you before he enters his final retreat. So you must take a second look at everything you see."

GRAY WOLF

Memory Walk

Are you a keen observer? Can you remember little details? Would you notice the color of an animal's fur or the shape its tail? If you are ready for a challenge, take a memory walk around your backyard, a local park, or even an overgrown vacant lot.

✔ Find a friend, parent, or other willing person to accompany you. Walk around silently for about five or ten minutes. Try to pay attention to everything you see. For example, you might notice a squirrel hopping about on the ground. Watch it carefully to see what it's doing. Listen to hear if it's making any sounds.

✔ When the time is up, ask each other questions about the things you saw, heard, or smelled. What color was that squirrel's fur? What did it do when it saw you?

✔ After quizzing each other, try to find answers to the questions you missed. Challenge yourselves to notice more each time you take a memory walk.

CANADA GOOSE
AND GOSLINGS

NINE-SPOTTED LADYBUG

WHITETAIL DEER TRACK

Chapter 2
Lessons for a Young Warrior

Ohiyesa's education couldn't be complete without spiritual training. Like other Sioux children, he learned that each leaf, each pebble, each whirring insect was part of the Great Mystery and therefore an object to be respected. He honored the Great Mystery by sitting quietly and thinking deeply about the power and greatness of nature.

Mysterious Medicine and Uncheedah trained him well. Ohiyesa was becoming a fine young warrior and hunter. Just before his fifteenth birthday, Mysterious Medicine gave Ohiyesa his first gun, an old flintlock. Possession of the rifle made him feel he was now old enough to join his uncle on the warpath. He still felt anger toward the whites who had killed his father and brothers. Solemnly he thought, "I shall soon be able to go among the whites whenever I wish, and to avenge the blood of my father and my brothers." It wasn't long before these strong feelings toward white people and their ways were tested.

One day in September 1872, Ohiyesa returned from a hunt to an unimaginable surprise. His father, whom everyone had thought was dead, was waiting for him at the camp! It was as if Ohiyesa's whole world was turned upside down. His father was alive, and so were his two older brothers.

After Many Lightnings's arrest, he had been sent to prison instead of being hanged. There he had converted to Christianity. When he was released from prison, he went to live on a reservation, or area set aside for Native Americans, on the Missouri River. Life was hard. There wasn't enough game on the reservation to feed the residents, so they depended on the U.S. government for food and money.

Along with a few others from the reservation, Many Lightnings decided to leave. A new law allowed Native Americans to apply for free land in unsettled areas, just as many whites were doing. Any person or family who promised to develop a ranch or farm and live on it would receive 160 acres of land. Many Lightnings started his homestead near the town of Flandreau, in Dakota Territory, and began to live like a white man. He even gave himself a white man's name: Jacob Eastman (Eastman was his wife's last name). Then he set out to find his family.

Ohiyesa listened as his father talked about the "civilized" life and how white men were religious and kindly. But none of it made sense. Why would his father choose to act and live like the white men who had mistreated him if he could return to the life he had always known? When Ohiyesa questioned his father, Jacob replied, "Our own life, I will admit, is the best in a world of our own, such as we enjoyed for ages. But . . . the sooner we accept [the whites'] mode of life and follow their teaching, the better it will be for us all."

Jacob convinced Ohiyesa and Uncheedah to return to the United States and settle on his farm. Trains roared across the prairies, and steamboats surged up the rivers. The world was changing, and Ohiyesa's life was too. Once more he was given a new name, Charles Alexander Eastman, though sometimes he would still use his Sioux name.

To live in the world of the white man, Charles needed to know how to read and write. Jacob dressed him in European-style pants and a shirt and sent him off to the nearby school. Without any knowledge of English, Charles was unable to understand anything his teacher said. When the other Indian students laughed at him, he ran out the door, determined to return to life in the woods.

His father understood Charles's shame but told him there was no going back. Jacob believed that the old days were dead and that the Sioux could survive only by changing. Charles must face school as if he were going on the warpath, his father explained. "I shall expect you to conquer." His father's devotion to this new way of life gradually won Charles over.

After two years in Flandreau, Charles went off to a mission school in Santee, Nebraska, many miles from his new home. Mission schools were set up by whites to teach Christianity to Native American children. So that they could read the Bible, they were also taught to read and write, both in their native language and in English. As Charles was leaving for Nebraska, his grandmother gave her blessing and some advice: "Always remember that the Great Mystery is good; evil can come only from ourselves."

Gradually Charles learned to speak, read, and act like a white person. In September 1876, Charles received word that his father had died. But Charles did what his father would have wanted and continued with his education.

Dr. Riggs, a Christian missionary and head teacher at Charles's school, had helped him get a scholarship to Beloit College, in Wisconsin, for the fall. Charles was eighteen years old, and the five-hundred-mile journey to Wisconsin filled him with wonder. He had never ridden a train or seen a large town or city before.

AMERICAN BISON

At first, Charles disliked living in Beloit. Only a few months earlier, Chief Sitting Bull and the Western Sioux had defeated General Custer in the battle of the Little Bighorn. Charles's uncles had taken part in the battle, and a false rumor spread around Beloit that Charles was the nephew of Sitting Bull himself. When Charles walked down the street, young boys would follow him, making war whoops. He felt like a stranger in strange country. Fortunately, most people in Beloit were kinder than they had first appeared. Soon Charles had many friends among the white students.

When Charles was twenty-one, Dr. Riggs helped him get another scholarship, this time to Knox College, in Illinois. Like most people his age, Charles thought a lot about his future. It seemed that having a definite profession would be helpful in this new life. What would his life's work be? He knew he wanted a career in which he could help his people, and finally he decided to become a doctor.

At Knox, Charles continued to do well at school, but he often missed his life in the wilderness. He found comfort and strength on long walks in the woods, especially at night. Others might have been nervous about what lurked in the dark, but Charles knew that if he was outside long enough, his eyes would adjust, no matter how inky black it was. Even without moonlight, he could distinguish the shapes of trees and the outline of the trail. In the silence, he listened to his own breathing and footfalls. He listened to the rustling of the leaves and could tell the difference between sounds made by the wind and sounds made by an animal. Since most mammals are **nocturnal,** or active at night, Charles often heard the calls of bats and other creatures. Sometimes he could even see their eyes gleaming in the starlight.

Bats (order Chiroptera)

39 species in North America

Habitat: caves, crevices, tree cavities, and buildings

Habits: nocturnal. Many species live in groups, but some are solitary. Some species hibernate during winter; others move south.

Nests: in ground burrows, tree cavities, or caves

Diet: Most species feed on flying insects, but some eat pollen or fruit.

RED BAT

Night Watch

Are you afraid of the dark? Ask a brave adult like your mom or dad to join you on a night journey into a dark or dimly lit backyard or park. You'll be so amazed by the sights and sounds, you may just forget your fears.

Supplies
flashlight
insect repellent (optional)

What to Do
✔ Find a comfortable place to stand or sit in the dark, and listen to the night sounds.

✔ Using your fingers, count all the different natural sounds you hear.

✔ Once your eyes adjust to the darkness, look around. Where are the sounds coming from? Can you see any animals? Can you recognize any familiar shapes in the dark?

✔ Before you go in for the night, switch on a flashlight and check out the surroundings. Were some of your guesses correct?

✔ Check out the same area in the daytime and study the shapes of the plants, rocks, and other things you see. The next time you do your night watch, see if you are any better at identifying the shapes and sounds around you.

During Charles's summer vacation in 1881, Dr. Riggs told him about Dartmouth College. Far across the country in New Hampshire, Dartmouth had been founded as a school for Indian youth. Now it was attended by the children of many rich and powerful white people, but those whites were still sympathetic to the plight of Native Americans and were interested in educating them. This college was a place where Charles could pursue his dream of becoming a doctor. Though he dreaded the thought of traveling so far from his friends and family, he decided to go east.

In January 1882, at age twenty-three, Charles boarded the train for Boston. As most Sioux were being pushed onto reservations out west, Charles was headed east to follow "the white man's trail." He was met at the station by Mr. and Mrs. Frank Woods, friends of Dr. Riggs. For the next few years, the couple looked after Charles, and he came to consider them his "white parents." They instructed him in the customs of city life and introduced him to people interested in helping Native Americans gain equality.

After taking some preparatory classes, Charles entered Dartmouth College in the fall of 1883. Students like Charles who were studying science had to take tough classes such as physics and chemistry.

They also had to learn to read science books in four languages besides English: French, German, Greek, and Latin. But Charles didn't give up. His grandmother had told him, "When you see a new trail, or footprint that you do not know, follow it to the point of knowing."

Charles (upper left) was a member of Dartmouth College's all-around athletic team.

20

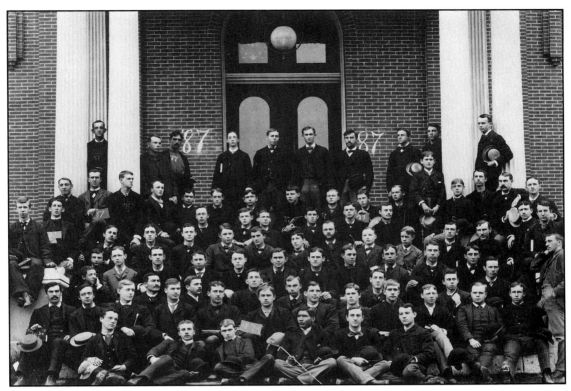

Dartmouth's class of 1887. Charles is in the front row, third from the right.

At Dartmouth, Charles met famous writers such as Ralph Waldo Emerson and Henry Wadsworth Longfellow. He played tennis and baseball and was captain of the football team. For three years, he held the college's long-distance running record. He became fascinated by the study of past civilizations. A bigger world had opened up to him.

In 1887, Charles graduated with honors and received a bachelor of science degree. With encouragement from Mr. and Mrs. Woods and other friends, he enrolled at Boston University's School of Medicine. He gained valuable experience working in Boston's South End, healing the poor. And in 1890, true to the prophecy at his birth, Charles became a "medicine man"—a doctor of medicine.

BLACKTAIL
PRAIRIE DOGS

Chapter 3
Old and New Trails

Upon graduation from Boston University, young Dr. Charles Eastman was offered a job as the physician at the Pine Ridge Reservation, in South Dakota. (South Dakota and North Dakota, formerly the Dakota Territory, had just become states in November 1889.) It had been a long time since Charles had been on the prairie. When he arrived in November 1890, the land looked barren and bleak compared to the lush forests of the East. The wind howled and blew dust everywhere. His clinic was a mess. Everything was coated with fine Dakota dust, and many basic supplies were missing. From the medical records, it was easy to see that the previous doctor had done little more than give out drugs to the Sioux people living on the reservation.

Soon Dr. Eastman had the clinic in order. He had six thousand people to look after, and many were sick. It was no wonder—crop failures and a disease among the cattle meant food was in short supply, and many people were hungry.

Charles as a medical student, 1890, and Elaine Goodale, 1891

Rather than just giving out drugs, Charles examined each of his patients carefully. He often traveled many miles on horseback in dangerous blizzards or blistering heat to check on them at their camps. Though he had been trained in "Western" medicine, he also respected the traditional Sioux healers and often worked in partnership with them. His hard work and respect for the old ways earned him the trust of his patients. It wasn't long before health conditions on the reservation began to improve.

The long days of work were tiring, but Charles was not too worn out to notice the pretty young supervisor of Sioux education, Elaine Goodale. She was from an educated white family out east. She had published a book of poetry as a child and recently had written articles about the education of Native Americans. During her years teaching at reservation schools, she had learned to speak Sioux and had taken to wearing moccasins. She respected many of the old ways but, like Charles's father, believed that Native Americans would need to learn the white people's way of life to survive.

Charles had read Elaine's writings, and she had heard of him from his brother John. They were immediately attracted to one another. Within a week of their first meeting, she accepted Charles's marriage proposal. Unfortunately, a few days after their engagement on Christmas Day, a tragedy occurred that would shock the nation and change their lives.

Feeling hungry and hopeless, many Sioux had embraced a new religion called the Ghost Dance religion. Started by a Paiute Indian holy man, it predicted that God would cause the downfall of white people and renew the strength of all Native Americans. Ghost Dancers sang and danced for the return of their dead ancestors and their old way of life. Even though the original Ghost Dancers preached nonviolence, reservation agents (white officials who ran the reservations) were scared by the popularity of the religion and banned it. But the Sioux kept dancing, and the religion spread from one reservation to another.

The agent in charge of Pine Ridge felt threatened by the Ghost Dancers and sent for soldiers from a nearby fort. Charles was against the presence of troops and told the agent that there was no plot among the Sioux to attack the whites. He believed the Sioux needed food, not soldiers. But the agent continued with his plan.

One of the armies was stationed at a camp on Wounded Knee Creek. On December 29, the cavalry encircled a group of Sioux who were fleeing their reservation after the death of Chief Sitting Bull. Sitting Bull had been shot by a white soldier as the chief was being arrested for his involvement with the Ghost Dance movement. The cavalry, afraid the Sioux might cause problems at Pine Ridge, began to take their guns away. Most of the visitors had already given up their guns when a shot rang out. Immediately the soldiers began to blast away with artillery at the entire crowd. Within a short time, 153 Sioux men, women, and children were dead. Twenty-five soldiers were killed, mostly from shots fired by their own troops.

Burying the dead after the Battle of Wounded Knee, S.D.-1890.

Elaine Goodale Eastman

Charles was placed in charge of caring for the wounded Sioux. With assistance from Elaine and others, he was able to save a few, but in the end, the death toll reached 200. Though Charles was thankful that he could be of service, he was horrified by the senseless murders.

In June 1891, after the pain of the massacre had eased, Elaine and Charles were married in New York City, where her father lived. On their way back to Pine Ridge, they stopped in Flandreau, South Dakota, where they were welcomed by Charles's brother John and almost the entire Sioux community.

It was early fall when the newlyweds returned to the reservation, and Charles started back to work. Elaine became his assistant. (She had resigned from her job with the Indian schools because of their trip east.) Congress had agreed to pay the Sioux at Pine Ridge for the losses of cattle and property that resulted from the army's actions at Wounded Knee. As the money was being given out, many of the Sioux complained that they were being cheated. Some spoke to Charles, and he tried to help, but he ended up getting himself into trouble with the agent at Pine Ridge.

Upset by the politics of working on a reservation, Charles soon resigned from his job. In 1893, the Eastmans and their newborn daughter, Dora, moved to St. Paul, Minnesota, where they opened a medical practice. It was hard to get new patients, probably because Charles was Sioux, and people wanted a white doctor. With few patients, Charles had a lot of extra time and began to do some writing. He wanted Dora to know about his early years, so he began to jot down stories of his days in the woods. Elaine liked the tales and sent the manuscripts to a children's magazine, *St. Nicholas,* which quickly agreed to publish them.

Nature Notes

Do you have nature stories to tell? One way of collecting material to build a story is to keep a nature journal.

Supplies
notebook
pencil

What to Do
Each time you watch animals, jot down some notes in a journal. Record the date and time of each observation. Over time, these field notes can reveal patterns of behavior. For example, your notes might show that your backyard squirrel collects acorns in the morning but is not to be seen at noon. What does it do at noon, and why does it collect acorns only in the morning? Does this mean it is solely **diurnal,** or can it be nocturnal too? Does it look for food every morning, or does it **hibernate** (sleep through the winter)? Questions like these are full of mystery. Mysteries make exciting reading and are fun to investigate.

Sometimes pictures can tell more than words. Why not illustrate your journal with drawings or even photos?

GRAY SQUIRREL
September 11
9:00 A.M.

Chewing on apples
in apple tree

In 1894, Charles was offered a job with the Young Men's Christian Association, or YMCA. The organization needed someone to establish YMCA chapters on Indian reservations and thought Charles would be the best person for the job. Charles accepted the offer and closed his medical practice. By teaching his people Christian values, he believed he could help them. Had not missionaries like Dr. Riggs helped him?

Soon Charles was traveling from one reservation to another. He talked to the men about the importance of keeping their bodies pure and healthy. He encouraged them to play lacrosse and polo for exercise. He warned them about the dangers of alcohol, tobacco, and gambling. Elaine supported his new work, although she had to spend a great deal of time alone with Dora and the Eastmans' new daughter, Irene.

On one of his trips, Charles was able to visit his uncle Mysterious Medicine, now a farmer and a Christian like Charles's father was. It had been twenty years since Charles had seen him, and they were both overjoyed. "The Great Spirit has been kind to let me see my boy again before I die," his uncle said as tears welled up in his eyes.

With Charles's help, there were soon forty-three YMCA chapters established among the Sioux, Cree, Ojibway, and Cheyenne. But other nations such as the Sac, Crow, and Fox rejected Christian beliefs. One old chief criticized white people for their disrespect of God and nature. He said they tore apart the land for gold and cut

down trees to build houses and churches. They seemed to think they could use these things to buy their way to Heaven, but the chief didn't think they even knew where Heaven was. Wasn't it right here in nature? "We shall still follow the old trail," he said. Charles accepted his wishes.

Charles and his daughter Dora, 1892

In 1900, Charles took a job as a reservation doctor at Crow Creek Agency, South Dakota. By this time, the Eastmans had two more children: Virginia was three and Charles Alexander II (called Ohiyesa) was two. (Dora was now seven and Irene five.) Charles did well at his new job, but once again he had problems with the agents running the reservation. After two and a half years, he quit.

For several years, Charles had been trying to help people on reservations collect payments owed to them by the government. Part of the problem was that the government's system required Native Americans to have a formal name in order to get a payment or a title to a piece of land. But like Charles, most Sioux had more than one name, and members of the same family did not have a common name to identify them as relatives. So the U.S. government hired Charles to assign each of the Sioux a first and last name that followed white people's standards.

Charles was sensitive to the significance of names. As he revised them, he tried hard to base them on the original Sioux names. For example, a man named Bobtailed Coyote was given the name Robert T. Wolf. A woman whose name meant She Who Has a Beautiful House was given the last name Goodhouse.

At first, many of the Sioux thought the renaming project was another plot to rob them of land and did not want to take "white" names. But once Charles explained how it was for their benefit, they agreed to assist him. During the six years that he worked on the project, Charles renamed over twenty-five thousand people.

GRIZZLY BEAR

BALD EAGLE

COYOTE

WHITETAIL DEER
FAWNS

Chapter 4
Stories to Tell

By the turn of the century, more and more Americans were living in cities. Smoke from factories blackened the skies. City streets echoed with the sounds of horses' hooves and smelled like manure. Alleys reeked of garbage, and rivers were used as sewers. Despite many modern conveniences, city life was often unpleasant. People were reading books such as *Wild Animals I Have Known,* by Ernest Thompson Seton, and *The Call of the Wild,* by Jack London, and dreaming of wild places. They began to think about protecting the remaining wild places left in America. Many naturalists joined together to start organizations that would protect animals. Even the president, Teddy Roosevelt, was a naturalist. He set aside land for new national parks, wildlife refuges, and forests.

As interest in nature grew, so did interest in traditional Native American ways. By this time, very few Native Americans were able to live a traditional life, because they had been pushed off their ancestors' lands. Nonetheless, that lifestyle fascinated city folk.

The stories Charles had written in the 1890s about his childhood became so popular that in 1902, they were published as a book, *Indian Boyhood.* This book was filled with real-life adventures from Charles's early days in the north woods of Minnesota and Manitoba. He even revealed some of his wildlife-watching tricks.

To attract chipmunks, Charles and his friends had learned to imitate the sounds they made. Sitting as still as statues in a clearing, some of the boys would use hollow stems of wild oats to chirp like chipmunks. After a while, curious chipmunks would creep out of their hiding places to see what was going on. When they entered the clearing, the other boys would leap from their hiding places among the trees and catch them.

Chipmunks (genuses *Eutamias* and *Tamias* in the family Sciuridae)

19 species in North America

Habitat: forests, brush, stream banks, deserts, and mountains

Habits: very active. Good tree climbers, often perching on branches to scold creatures below. Hibernate in winter

Nests: in burrows or tree cavities

Diet: seeds, berries, nuts, insects, grasses, meat, and bird eggs

LEAST CHIPMUNK

In 1904, Charles published a book that presented Native American attitudes about animals. *Red Hunters and the Animal People* included animal tales and hunters' real accounts of animal behavior. One hunter told about a deer that saved herself from a hungry wolf by luring it into a pond and then kicking it to death with her front hooves. Another hunter shared his observations about the alarm calls of wild animals. "It is well known that the alarm call of the loon, the crane, and the wild goose is understood by all of the winged people that swim the lakes. This is not all. Many of the four-footed people of the woods know it as well. It often happens when I hunt waterfowl that one gives the alarm and immediately all the ducks swim out, away from the shore. Those that cannot swim crouch down to conceal themselves, and even small animals stealthily and swiftly dodge back into the woods."

Often when a bird or mammal notices a **predator** such as a wolf or weasel or owl, it will utter a distinctive alarm call that other animals understand. Those animals may join in with distress signals of their own. Like a security system, this wild ruckus often spoils a hunter's chance of making a surprise attack.

SPARROW

SHORTTAIL WEASEL

Psssh!

When you know how to imitate alarm calls, you can attract curious animals on the lookout for danger. Two simple alarm notes are "peeshing" and the "kiss chirp." Peeshing is an imitation of the alarm call of wrens and squirrels. The kiss chirp sounds something like the distress notes of chipmunks and sparrows. Other animals such as marmots and ground squirrels may emit a loud whistle.

What to Do

✔ Sit as motionless as a boulder in a quiet, outdoor location.

✔ To peesh, make a very loud shhhh sound while opening and closing your lips. To produce the kiss chirp, just make a series of loud, puckery kisses on the palm of your hand.

✔ Pick one sound and stick with it for a few minutes. Glance about as you call, and perhaps you'll see some curious neighborhood birds and animals trying to spot the dangerous hunter.

✔ Whenever you're outside, keep tuned to alarm calls. Most likely they are announcing the presence of a predator such as an owl or weasel, and you may have an opportunity to see one of these secretive hunters. On the other hand, the calls could also be warning others about you!

Native American hunters had long studied the ways of animals and shared their observations with each other. Charles Eastman's books showed white people how Native Americans studied wildlife and how they passed on their knowledge to their children.

These books fascinated readers. They were translated into other languages and widely read in Europe. Charles was invited to give lectures all over the U.S. His family had grown to include six children, and Elaine stayed home with them while he attended important events and met famous people such as author Mark Twain and civil rights activist W. E. B. Du Bois. Charles had followed many trails since his early days in the Minnesota woods. In writing about nature, he had chosen a path that allowed him to celebrate and share his Native American roots.

MOUNTAIN LION

BLACK BEAR
IN WHITE
PINE TREE

Chapter 5
Camp Days

Charles met many famous naturalist-writers, but the one to whom he became closest was Ernest Thompson Seton. Unlike some popular writers of animal books, Seton based his stories on real observation. He spent hours out-of-doors, watching and sketching wild creatures. He was fascinated by the traditions of Native Americans and wanted other white people to respect native cultures.

Seton was very excited when he read Charles's books, because he thought it was important for young people to learn outdoor skills and Native American values. In 1902, Seton had started a youth organization called the Woodcraft Indians, which quickly spread throughout the country. It was exciting for young white children to learn about the old ways of Native Americans. At camp, they learned to track animals, make a shelter, and perform other outdoor skills. In 1910, Seton helped found the Boy Scouts of America. The Boy Scouts was a blend of the Woodcraft Indians and the English Boy Scouts, which had a military focus. A similar organization, the Camp Fire Girls, was also cofounded by Seton. Soon after he was elected chairman of the Boy Scouts of America, Seton invited Charles to help him develop the scouting program.

Ernest Thompson Seton, shown here in 1930

Charles was made a national councilman and director of a scout camp. He wrote articles for the scouting magazine *Boy's Life*, and in 1914, he published a guide for Boy Scouts and Camp Fire Girls called *Indian Scout Talks* (later renamed *Indian Scout Craft and Lore*). "To be in harmony with nature," the book began, "one must be true in thought, free in action, and clean in body, mind, and spirit." Charles's vision of scouting was a blend of Native American tradition and the values of Christian groups like the YMCA. He was sharing what he had learned from his elders and passing it down to kids across America who were growing up in cities and towns. Young people were ready for scouting, and soon there were troops in many communities.

In the summer of 1915, Elaine and Charles opened a camp for girls at Granite Lake, in New Hampshire. It was called the School of the Woods, and it offered sports and nature activities. The three eldest Eastman children became camp counselors. Dora had just graduated from Mount Holyoke College, and Irene and Virginia were still college students. Even the three younger children, Charles II, Eleanor, and Florence, helped with camp chores.

Forming an Adventure Team

You don't have to be a scout to scout about for wild critters. Do you know other kids who are interested in wildlife? Next time you encounter a fellow wildlife watcher (it could even be a brother, a sister, or a parent!), team up on your animal explorations. Perhaps you can share books, tools, or most important, your ideas. Together, keep a list of the different animals you spot in your neighborhood. Post the list in an obvious place, such as on your refrigerator door. Add the names of any new sightings, then compare your list with that of your teammate. If you have access to a computer with on-line capabilities, you can even link up with wildlife watchers in other parts of the country.

Charles leads an archery class at Camp Oahe.

The School of the Woods was a success. The next summer, the Eastmans changed its name to Camp Oahe and opened a second camp, Camp Ohiyesa, for boys. The campers were taught as Charles had been. Though they didn't hunt, they learned to understand signs left by animals. They even learned to examine and identify **scats,** or animal droppings.

Foxes (part of the family Canidae)

4 species in North America

Habitat: found in a variety of habitats, from forests to deserts. Red and gray foxes are the most common and are found throughout much of the United States.

Habits: mostly nocturnal. Active all winter

Dens: in ground burrows or tree cavities

Diet: mostly small mammals, but also seeds, fruit, insects, birds, and eggs

GRAY FOX

RED FOX

As a boy, Charles had learned that scats were a sign of great importance to the hunter. An examination of a scat could reveal not only which animal had been in the area, but what it had eaten and how long ago it had passed by.

Dropped Clues

If you consider yourself a bold explorer, you can gross out your friends and shock your parents by checking out the neighborhood scats. Though it may seem a little disgusting to examine animal scat, it's really not too bad once you try it. Most scats don't smell, especially old, dry ones. It's best not to touch them with your bare hands, though. Use a stick to break up a scat, then look closely for clues to the animal's diet (a hand lens can help). In a fox scat, it's possible to find everything from cricket legs to berry seeds to mouse jaws, while in a lizard scat, you can find the parts of a variety of insects. Most field guides to animal tracks can help you tell one kind of scat from another.

WARNING: Keep your distance from cat and dog scats. These can sometimes be the source of unpleasant infections. And be sure to wash your hands well after any scatological adventure.

With the patience of a great teacher, Charles taught campers all about observing animals. He shared his respect for wild creatures and his belief that they can sense when people intend to harm them. He cautioned the children against paying too much attention to adventure stories that overdramatized the dangers in nature. Telling stories from his own youth, he emphasized the gentleness of wild creatures (with the exception of the grizzly bear!). As the children watched animals in the wild, Charles pointed out how they minded their own business and didn't usually bother people unless people bothered them.

Even in the woods around the camps, it was not always easy to find wild animals. Many creatures, such as opossums, bobcats, and raccoons, are nocturnal, so the best time to see them is when most people are sleeping. One way to discover the nighttime antics of these critters is to learn how to read their tracks. As a young hunter, Charles had learned how to read tracks the way you have learned to read words. At his camps and in his books, he explained the language of footprints.

"The footprint . . . is first of all a picture of all the prominent points on the sole. The ball of the foot, the heel and toes, hoof and claw, each makes its own impress. Even the fishes make theirs with their fins, which to them are hand and foot. This is the wood-dweller's autograph."

For example, a raccoon foot is distinguished by its five toes, which make it look like a miniature human hand. Pairs of the footprints appear side by side, because a raccoon places its left hind foot beside its right forefoot as it lumbers along.

Raccoon (*Procyon lotor*)

Habitat: along streams and lakes near wooded areas, in suburban parks, and in old houses

Habits: nocturnal. May stay in its den during cold spells but does not hibernate

Dens: in burrows, rock crevices, or tree cavities

Diet: seeds, fruit, insects, small animals and birds, frogs, snails, crayfish, bird eggs, and trash. May dunk food in water before eating

On the Right Track

The easiest way to find out who your nocturnal neighbors are is to make a track area of your own and lure them with a tasty tidbit or two.

Supplies
tarp or old sheet at least 6 ft. by 6 ft.
fine sand or soil
shovel
rake
hose with spray nozzle
wheelbarrow or bucket
fruit and vegetable scraps
guide to animal tracks

RACCOON (FRONT FOOT)

What to Do
✔ Pick a flat surface near your home. A lawn or sidewalk might do (ask an adult for permission first). Lay out the tarp or sheet.

✔ Shovel some sand or soil into a wheelbarrow or bucket and empty it onto the tarp.

✔ Use the flat side of the rake to spread a 1- to 2-inch layer of soil or sand over it.

✔ Spray the surface with water until it is just wet. Try to avoid making puddles.

✔ Before you go to sleep, check to see that the soil or sand is still wet. Toss some fruit and vegetable scraps into the center of the track area.

✔ Check out the area in the morning. Can you see any tracks?

✔ If you don't have a knowledgeable teacher like Charles Eastman available to help, use an animal-track field guide to help you identify your visitors.

NOTE: Do not do this activity in a park or nature preserve where feeding animals is against the rules. Also, don't make a habit of leaving food scraps out—your neighbors might not appreciate the new traffic, and animals may come to depend on your help instead of looking for food themselves.

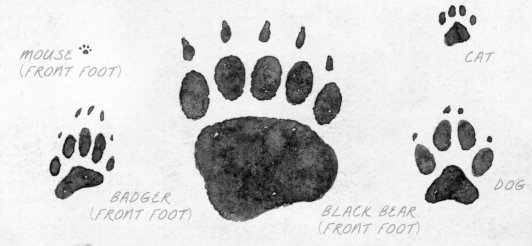

MOUSE 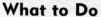 (FRONT FOOT)

CAT

BADGER (FRONT FOOT)

BLACK BEAR (FRONT FOOT)

DOG

Many animals will follow well-worn trails to feeding areas or water. These trails are narrower than human paths and often go under low branches. The smaller the animal, the narrower its trail. Tiny creatures like meadow mice make paths no wider than your big toe. Animals' trails often lead to their burrows or nests, but as Charles Eastman wrote, they sometimes lead elsewhere. "Many animals for safety's sake go through a series of manoeuvers before they lie down to rest. For instance, at the end of the trail they make two loops, and conceal themselves at a point where the pursuer must, if he sticks to the trail, pass close by their hiding-place and give timely warning of his approach. This trick is characteristic of the deer and rabbit families."

Rabbits and Hares (family Leporidae)

17 species in North America

Habitat: brush, weed patches, grasslands, forests, and sometimes swamps and deserts

Habits: most species active at night and throughout winter

Nests: in burrows or tree cavities (rabbits) or in high grass or brush (hares)

Diet: leaves, berries, and bark

EASTERN COTTONTAIL (RABBIT)

WHITETAIL JACKRABBIT (HARE)

Tracking Tips

Test your track-reading skills by looking in fields, forests, or other areas where wildlife may be abundant. The muddy or sandy banks of ponds and streams are a good place to see tracks. In the winter, they are easy to find right after a fresh snowfall.

✔ **Trail Markers**

Scats sometimes serve as trail markers, because many animals, such as deer and coyotes, eliminate waste wherever they are. When you come across a scat, check to see if it's on a trail.

✔ **Follow That Track**

Following tracks can lead you to further clues and sometimes, if they are fresh and you are quiet, to the animal itself. Tracks that disappear at the base of a tree may belong to a tree-climbing critter such as a squirrel or chipmunk. Beware of following large footprints that lead to a cave—they may belong to a bear!

✔ **Read the Signs**

The outdoors are full of signs of wildlife. Unlike stop signs or no-parking signs, these signs lack words. Look on the ground for places where an animal such as a skunk may have poked about looking for worms or beetles.

Scan tree trunks for areas where the bark has been chewed off. If it's high on the tree, it was probably the work of a porcupine. Search for bits of fur or feathers on the ground. These are signs of a struggle between animals. Read up on animals that live in your area to learn more about their behavior, and you'll discover more signs to look out for.

PORCUPINE

In 1918, Elaine and the Eastmans' daughters caught the Spanish flu. All of them recovered except Irene, who died on October 23. Heartbroken, the Eastmans buried Irene under a tree at their summer camp.

The Eastmans continued to operate their camps for a few more years, and Charles actively fought for the rights of Native Americans.

Just as Charles used both his Sioux and his English names, he wore both traditional Native American dress and the typical white man's fashions comfortably.

Although many Native Americans, including Charles's son, served as soldiers in World War I, they were not citizens in their own land. Those like Charles who had assumed the white lifestyle could vote and hold government jobs. But they could not run for a political office or practice their religion and customs openly. Those living on reservations had no rights at all. Other people born in the United States were given citizenship, Charles protested. Why not Native Americans?

Since his first lecture as a college student, Charles had enjoyed speaking before audiences, and now his lectures were in demand. He captivated crowds with his rich voice and unusual appearance. Often he dressed in traditional Sioux clothes, including a richly feathered war bonnet. However, it was Charles's message, not his looks, that attracted listeners. Dr. Eastman had lived in two extremely different cultures, and he shared his insights from both. Once, while speaking to a crowd that included many big-game hunters, he shared how he had grown up with animals—even sleeping and eating with a pet baby grizzly bear. (Don't try that at home!) He criticized the people in many frontier towns who quickly killed wild creatures they saw, whether the animals were a threat or not. He spoke of the respect that the Native American hunter had for the life of each animal he killed and how none of the animal's parts went to waste—not even the hooves and bones. Charles also shared his people's concern about the way settlers were cutting down forests, tearing up the earth, and dumping garbage and sewage into waterways. To the Sioux, the destruction of nature was a terrible act.

Habitat Protectors

Since Charles Eastman's days, the amount of wild land where animals can freely roam has grown smaller and smaller. Though you may see some critters near towns and cities, many creatures depend on the little islands of wilderness protected in parks or wildlife preserves. Large animals such as deer and mountain lions need large territories in order to survive. Here are some ways you can help.

✔ Land Savers

Work with people in your community to set aside parks or greenbelts where wildlife can live in peace. Nationwide programs also work to preserve wildlife habitats. A good one is the Backyard Habitat Program sponsored by the National Wildlife Federation. To request information on this program, write to the National Wildlife Federation, Backyard Habitat Program, 8925 Leesburg Pike, Vienna, VA 22184. Ask for packet #79946. You can also learn about this and other National Wildlife Federation programs by visiting their World Wide Web site: http://www.nws.org/nwf.

✔ Wildlife Garden

The lawns, concrete, and asphalt that surround many of our homes create a setting that's a wildlife wasteland. Turn your backyard or local vacant lot into a miniature jungle by planting native flowers, trees, and shrubs. (Check out a nursery or look through a regional plant guide for some ideas, and ask for permission if the land isn't yours.) These will provide wild animals with seeds and fruits that they depend upon for food.

✔ Home Sweet Homes

Many animals require tree cavities to nest in. If you don't have any big old trees in your neighborhood, buy or make nest boxes. Shrubs and brush piles also make popular homes.

✔ Bath Time

If you have the space, make a shallow cement pool where creatures can come to drink or take a bath.

WHITETAIL DEER BUCK

COTTONTAIL RABBITS

In 1921, after thirty years of marriage, Charles and Elaine decided to separate. They had grown apart over the years and wanted to live their own lives. For a few years, Charles traveled around the country, inspecting the conditions on reservations for the U.S. government. In 1928, at the age of seventy, he toured England, giving speeches about Native American culture. Though he enjoyed the status of well-known author and lecturer, Charles preferred to spend most of his last years at a cabin he had built on the Canadian shore of Lake Huron. There he could canoe and swim in the cold waters. He could hunt and fish and, best of all, get acquainted with all his animal neighbors.

Charles devoted his last years to quiet contemplation of nature. He believed there were many secrets to learn from wild animals. He recognized that the way he learned about animals was entirely different from the "European" naturalist. "We [Native Americans] do not chart and measure the vast field of nature or express her wonders in terms of science," wrote Charles. "On the contrary, we see miracles on every hand—the miracle of the life in seed and egg, the miracle of death in a lightning flash and the swelling deep."

Charles Eastman was many things in his life. He was a young warrior, a doctor, a missionary, a writer, a government worker, and a spokesman for Native Americans. At the age of seventy-five, Charles was awarded a medal from the Indian Council Fire (a national Native American organization) for his achievements.

Despite failing health, Charles continued to travel, write, and spend time alone at his cabin. In January 1939, while visiting his son in Detroit, he suffered a heart attack and died. The man known as Hakadah, Ohiyesa, and Dr. Charles Eastman had followed many trails and left many messages for us to learn from. Like Charles Eastman, you too can live a rich life among your wild neighbors and draw wisdom from the mysteries of nature.

BLACK BEAR SKULL
AMIDST BLUEBERRY
GROWTH

Important Dates

1858—Hakadah (eventually known as Charles Alexander Eastman) is born in February near Redwood Falls, Minnesota.

1862—Receives a new name, Ohiyesa. Sioux uprising forces family to leave for Canada. Father and brothers are believed dead

1872—Father reappears, brings Ohiyesa back to Dakota Territory

1876–1879—Attends Beloit College

1879–1881—Attends Knox College

1883–1887—Attends Dartmouth College

1887–1890—Attends Boston University School of Medicine

1890—Takes physician job at the Pine Ridge Indian Reservation

1891—Marries Elaine Goodale

1892—Daughter Dora is born

1893—Opens medical practice in St. Paul, Minnesota

1894—Daughter Irene is born

1894—Goes to work for the Young Men's Christian Association (YMCA)

1897?—Daughter Virginia is born

1898?—Son Charles II (also called Ohiyesa) is born

1900—Takes a position as doctor at the Crow Creek Agency, South Dakota

1902?—Daughter Eleanor is born (The birth year of the Eastmans' youngest daughter, Florence, is not known.)

1902—Publishes *Indian Boyhood*

1903—Begins renaming project, moves to Amherst, Massachusetts

1904—Publishes *Red Hunters and the Animal People*

1910—Begins association with the Boy Scouts and the Camp Fire Girls

1911—Publishes *The Soul of an Indian*

1914—Publishes *Indian Scout Talks: A Guide for Boy Scouts and Camp Fire Girls* (later renamed *Indian Scout Craft and Lore*)

1915—Opens the School of the Woods

1916—Publishes *From the Deep Woods to Civilization*

1918—Daughter Irene dies

1921—Separates from Elaine

1928—Moves to a cabin on Lake Huron

1939—Dies of a heart attack on January 8

BEAVER LODGE

COMMON LOON

Glossary

diurnal: active during the daytime

hibernate: to pass the winter in a deep sleep

mammal: any type of animal whose young are fed with mother's milk

naturalist: a person who studies nature

nocturnal: active during the nighttime

predator: an animal who hunts and eats other animals

scats: animal droppings

species: a group of plants or animals that are able to breed with one
another

Bibliography

Anderson, H. Allen. *The Chief: Ernest Thompson Seton and the Changing West.* College Station, Tex.: Texas A&M Press, 1986.

Eastman, Charles Alexander. *From the Deep Woods to Civilization: Chapters in the Autobiography of an Indian.* Lincoln: University of Nebraska Press, 1977.

*———. *Indian Boyhood.* New York: Dover Publications, 1971.

*———. *Indian Scout Craft and Lore.* New York: Dover Publications, 1974.

———. *Red Hunters and the Animal People.* New York: AMS Press, 1976.

———. *The Soul of an Indian.* Edited by Kent Nerburn. San Rafael, Calif.: New World Library, 1994.

Graber, Kay, ed. *Sister to the Sioux: The Memoirs of Elaine Goodale Eastman, 1885–91.* Lincoln: University of Nebraska Press, 1978.

Meyer, Roy W. *History of the Santee Sioux: United States Indian Policy on Trial.* Lincoln: University of Nebraska Press, 1967.

Nabakov, Peter. *Native American Testimony: A Chronicle of Indian-White Relations from Prophecy to the Present, 1492-1992.* New York: Viking, 1991.

Wilson, Raymond. *Ohiyesa: Charles Eastman, Santee Sioux.* Urbana: University of Illinois Press, 1983.

*An asterisk denotes material for younger readers.

Index